Another Way

Navigating Toward Positive

Change

by

Joanna Moore

Another Way: Navigating Toward Positive Change

© 2022 by Joanna Malaczynski-Moore

All rights reserved.

Cover art by Joanna Malaczynski-Moore © 2022

Acknowledgements

This book could not have been written without the efforts of countless philosophers, spiritual teachers and others who came before me. Throughout the course of history they have helped preserve our understanding of what it means to be human and to navigate this world. (The Resources and Inspiration Section at the end of this book highlights the thinkers that have most influenced me.)

I am also grateful to all of the individuals who have supported my efforts to affect change over the years, including my family, friends, and mentors. You have made it possible for me to run a number of experiments in this world and take the time to learn as much as possible about how we navigate change. I also wish to thank all of the people who have resisted my efforts to change anything. You have also taught me many lessons about this world.

A special thanks to author Ray Pace, who reached out to me and encouraged me to self-publish as an indie publisher.

For the video course accompaniment to this book,

please visit my website at:

joannamoore.com

Introduction

When I was in graduate school studying environmental sustainability, professionals out in the field would visit our classes, telling us that we have to change the world because they were not able to. They would look at our work, get excited about our vision, and tell us that this was exactly what the world needed. It never occurred to me to ask these professionals why they were not able to change the world. I just assumed it was because they did not have the know-how that we would bring to the table.

Upon graduation, I joined the ranks of professionals who were excited about making the world a better place. However, I found that I was not able to make a meaningful impact; nor was anyone else. Not because we did not try, but because many of our colleagues and clients were largely resistant to change—directly or inadvertently. Indeed, some of the individuals who hired me to work on sustainability projects became my greatest opponents. And the clients who approached us based on our sustainability work would frequently backpedal away from meaningful commitment.

The roadblocks were ones of human psychology, rather than a lack of technology or shortage of funding. That became very clear to me over the years as I watched opportunities come and go in a diversity of contexts. Despite these insights, I became highly demoralized by my inability to affect change. I had invested myself professionally into this effort, foregoing a career and a much better salary as an attorney. I felt that I had accomplished very little despite the investments I had made, and that I had taken a wrong turn professionally.

Feeling paralyzed by my own confusion, I turned to spirituality and other disciplines to help me figure out what had happened and to sort out the disappointment that I felt personally and professionally as a result of my failed efforts. In the process of examining my own predicament, I came to realize that our capacity to solve our problems is dependent upon effective use of our internal navigation system. Our internal navigation system guides us through both our own personal problems and our global problems as a society.

This book is a culmination of what I learned about the role of our internal navigation system in affecting change. I sought out as much information as possible on how we are most and least effective utilizing that system, tapping into the fields of spirituality, philosophy, psychology, anthropology, user experience design, and the law. It does not matter if you are reading this book because you are going through a life transition or because you are trying to change the world. The decision-making process and internal navigation that needs to take place in each case is the same.

Chapter 1: Our Navigation System

We get accustomed to the way things are, regardless of whether we want or do not want anything different. We may not even like the status quo, but we are inevitably habituated toward some aspects of it. It may be the financial security it offers. The social stability it provides us. The emotional certainty it exerts upon us. As a result we become paralyzed when we are faced with anything undesirable or unexpected. We struggle, become frustrated, and start to feel lost.

Change is rarely a straightforward process and we are likely to face the undesirable and unexpected along the way. We can navigate through change successfully if we make full use of our basic biology, which wires us to effectively navigate the world. That biology is made up of our beliefs, emotions, senses, and thoughts. These work in tandem so that we can acknowledge emerging conditions, evaluate them, and take responsive action.

Our biological navigation systems are mostly out of practice because in our modern culture we do not utilize our senses effectively, we do not process our emotions fully, and because we are prone to intellectual denial. What makes matters worse is that in adopting the norms of our modern society—along with its belief systems and modes of operating—we actively hijack our navigation system. All of this prevents us from moving toward positive change—as individuals and as a society.

This book will take you on a personal journey and tour of your internal navigation system. You will get to delve deeply into the change you are facing or hoping to create. Chapters 2-4 will explore the subject of what motivates you. Chapters 5-6 will explain how you are intellectually vulnerable to getting lost in denial. Chapters 7-9 will introduce you to some of the most underutilized aspects of your internal navigation system. Chapters 10-15 will demonstrate how you can utilize that system properly to engage with whatever reality you are facing. Chapters 16-17 will tackle two major cultural constructs that hijack your navigation system. Finally, Chapters 18-20 will address how you can best interact with others.

Take your time doing the journaling / meditation exercises at the end of each chapter. They will help you develop the intellectual resiliency and strength to create change and successfully navigate through difficult situations. I suggest that you write three pages journaling answers to each question and meditate upon your answers. This may sound excessive to you, but it is not. You might be halfway through page two or need to spend a few days thinking about or feeling into your answers before you gain clarity. So give yourself the time and space to do so.

Journaling / Meditation Questions

1. Think of a situation in which you initiated change. Did your expectations of how things would unfold deviate from reality?

2. Think of a situation in which change came to you. Who initiated the change? How did it affect you?

3. Think of a situation where you avoided change. What were you avoiding? What was the outcome?

Chapter 2: Motivating Needs

We are tied to the status quo because it helps meet our needs. When enough of our needs are not being met, we will long for something different. If our needs are being threatened by emerging circumstances, we will resist change. Our needs are motivators and will determine whether we desire or resist movement.

Human beings have a common set of needs. They fall into seven categories, and all of them are about how we feel. To various degrees, we want to feel that we are:

1. Safe and secure
2. Accomplishing our goals
3. In control of our lives
4. Understood, accepted, belonging
5. Autonomous individuals
6. Enjoying our lives
7. Making a positive impact on the world

We form priorities with respect to these seven categories based on our personal experiences and the experiences of others we identify with. For example, we may have experienced a period of time when we lost flexibility in our work schedule (part of our autonomy); as a result, we may prioritize maintaining or regaining that flexibility going forward. It is also possible that we got lucky at some point and our need for autonomy was fulfilled so well that the experience formed a clear impression in our mind that we want more of the same. Alternatively, we may have witnessed other people experience certain positive or negative events with respect to getting their needs met, and this has left a strong impression on us about what we most value.

We will also sometimes be put in a position where external constraints force us to make a decision to prioritize one of our needs above others. For example, we may have to choose between having a sense of belonging with others and our sense of autonomy. We will not be happy being forced to choose. However, such decision points help us refine our understanding of what we most need at any given time, by getting us to focus our attention and energies on what is most important to us.

We can learn a lot about ourselves by seeing what we choose to sacrifice when we are forced to make tough decisions. Indeed, our priorities will reveal a tremendous amount of information about how we approach various types of change in our lives.

How we perceive any emerging situation—and the emotional response we have to it— depends upon whether we perceive that our needs, as prioritized, are being met or displaced by it. Take, for example, two individuals with different priorities who interpreted the same changing circumstances at work very differently: both were told that their companies would move everyone to a work from home situation.

The first person lived in the US, had a long driving commute, worked in a cubicle, and had little occasion to socialize with their colleagues. They were thrilled to be working from home and overjoyed at their company's decision. It offered them more flexibility and free time. Their conclusion was that the change created an opportunity for their company to realize that its employees were equally productive working remotely.

The second person lived in Europe, walked to work, engaged with their teammates at the office, and it was custom for them to take social breaks and lunches with their colleagues. They were mortified by their company's decision to move to a work from home situation. It would strip them of a large part of their connection to others. Their conclusion was that their company was trying to isolate and control its workforce and that the change was just an excuse to do that.

The difference between the two individuals and their interpretation of reality is that one lived within a context in which the change to working at home felt like something positive had been granted to them (flexibility and free time) based on their priorities. The second person lived within a context in which the same change felt like something positive has been taken away from them (professional connection and social contact) based on a totally different set of priorities. The example illustrates that the way in which we judge our reality is dependent on whether we feel that our needs, as currently prioritized, are being threatened or fulfilled by the changing situation.

Journaling / Meditation Questions

1. What needs of yours do you believe will be fulfilled by the changing situation?

2. What needs of yours do you believe will be undermined by the changing situation?

3. What perspective and motivations are you attributing to others around this situation? Why?

4. Are you being forced to choose between one need and another? Which one do you choose and why?

Chapter 3: Alternative Plans and Desires

How we choose to pursue our needs defines our desires. One person may desire to fulfill their need for companionship by joining a sports team. Another person may desire to fulfill that same need by joining a book group. Our desires are a function of our individual preferences, past experiences, assumptions and belief systems.

We may think that our current desire is the only way to meet our needs, but there are always a number of options. And this is one of the most difficult things for us to understand, especially when the going gets tough. We become extremely vested in our desires because our minds set up a narrow range of circumstances under which we believe our needs can be met. If we do not obtain our object of desire, we are frustrated, feel defeated and may even enter a state of panic.

Our modern culture encourages us to fulfill our desires through control. It teaches us that if we are not working hard or trying harder, we must be lazy or incompetent. As a result, we start planning out in great detail how our desires should be fulfilled, including the specific steps we must take and in what order. We then enslave ourselves to executing those plans, regardless of what comes our way. When we hit road blocks, we cannot and will not see any other alternatives because of our control-oriented work ethic.

Control becomes a creativity killer because we become so dead-set on things unfolding a specific way. We become paralyzed by our plans and expectations, and cannot come up with anything else when reality does not unfold the way we expected. We cling on to our ideas of how things should be, rather than recognizing how they really are and working within that reality.

Our plans are based on our beliefs and assumptions about the world and how it works. If we believe we must get a specific degree in order to work in a certain field, it will not be possible for us to work in that field if we do not pursue the degree. And if anything disrupts our ability to get that degree, we will be crushed by our belief that we will never accomplish our goal. We will also have a hard time being open to the idea that we can pursue other occupations that would land us in the same or similar field, for example.

Our subjective beliefs and assumptions are generally built upon an intellectual house of cards. This house of cards is based on our limited life experiences, other people's opinions, what our culture believes, and what we learn from the media. We are not used to seeing our plans as a house of cards. And rarely do we realize that there could be ways of getting our needs met that do not follow our grand plans. Instead, we see our plans as necessary and essential for accomplishing our goals. We stick to our plans and seek to fit the world into an intellectual box that meets our expectations of how things should unfold.

Unfortunately (and fortunately), an infinite number of factors can influence whether the events we expect will ever happen, how they will happen, and whether they are prerequisites for getting our needs met. And we cannot foresee the future—nor can we control when or how any of these things will happen to us in a consistent manner. We are just one entity in a soup of many forces out there that will determine how things play out.

Even if we know this intellectually, we seek to control in the first place because we fear the consequences of not having our needs fulfilled. When we live in such fear and are wedded to our grand plans as a control-maintenance strategy, any unmet expectation or desire can cause us to fall into a panic. Ultimately we fear that if our needs are not met, we will be miserable—specifically, that we will feel lonely, be humiliated, starve, etc. Indeed, what we fear most is the pain we anticipate we will feel if our needs go unfulfilled.

Journaling / Meditation Questions

1. What do you desire?

2. What are your underlying needs behind those desires? Refer to the seven categories of needs listed at the beginning of Chapter 2 for guidance.

3. What do you fear will happen if your desires are not fulfilled? What needs of yours will not be met?

4. What do you fear will happen if your needs go unfulfilled? How will you feel?

Chapter 4: Beliefs & Assumptions

Our brain is charged with thinking so that we can move toward or away from a situation, depending on whether we believe it will fulfill or undermine our needs. We figure out how to get access to the food, shelter, love, acceptance, and numerous other resources we sense to be out there in this world. However, whether we believe a given situation will take us closer to or further away from getting our needs met depends on our assumptions.

Because each of us has a limited understanding of our world, and limited control over how it will unfold, all we can do is make assumptions about what we think is relevant to us and how we think things will play out. Frequently, these assumptions will not be accurate. They may have been accurate in the past or may hold true under certain circumstances, but they may not be accurate in the present moment. This is because our assumptions tend to be a narrow representation of the feasible experiences available in this world and are based on our limited experiences in and understanding of it. In other words, the world is much broader and a lot more options are possible than we can ever realize.

Often times when we project our assumptions onto a situation, we become resistant to seeing and accepting that situation as it really is. Our version of reality is clouded by not only our personal experiences, but also the experiences of our friends, family, mentors, and anyone else whose ideas we have internalized into our belief system. For most people that includes messaging from social media, films and TV, and other ideas we have been consuming since we were kids. We hold on to our beliefs and assumptions like they are the law of the land, even though they are often not accurate.

Our beliefs and assumptions are handy tools to help us navigate a complex world because we cannot possibly take in all of its complexity at once. We therefore approximate the state of the world with our assumptions in order to make it possible for us to navigate through it. We would be non-functional without our beliefs and assumptions, as well as the expectations and judgments that result from them. They are necessary to gauge the world in front of us with each step that we take. However, when we are in an emerging situation, we have a hard time seeing our options clearly because we are limited by our existing beliefs and assumptions. We eliminate options from consideration because they are at odds with what we currently believe is feasible, true, or the right thing to do.

The most challenging thing about our beliefs and assumptions is that we usually do not even know that we have them. We do not consciously realize that we are operating on a theoretical model of the world. Instead we move forward as if we are seeing reality just as it really is and following immutable laws. Things get even more complicated when our thoughts, feelings, words and actions are based on layers of assumptions.

The house of cards that is our mental model of the world gets even more tenuous.

Being conscious of our beliefs and assumptions is critical for successfully engaging with the world, especially under changing circumstances or when things are not going our way. One way to do that is to write down our logic or reasoning with respect to our expectations and actions. When doing this, place any and all thoughts you have in one of three categories: (1) knowns or things you immutably know to be true; (2) unknowns or things you would like to find out; and (3) assumptions or things you presume, hope, or suppose are true.

Each time you write something in the "knowns" list, I recommend that you check again. Do you really know that it is true? Are you certain it is true? How do you know it is true? Is it only true under certain circumstances and not others? If your knowns statements have any of the following words in them, you need to be especially cautious: always, all, never, no one, every time, should. "No one ever listens to me." "He is always late." "They never inform me of what is going on." "Every time I try to talk to her about it, she brushes me off." "They always know what's best." "You should't think that." Such absolute statements are ripe for rebuttal.

Our beliefs and assumptions need to be validated for accuracy, rather than be taken as fact. This means asking questions (as discussed in Chapter 19), doing some research, and using our senses to more fully observe the world (as discussed in Chapters 7-8). Frequently, assumptions will hold true under one context but not another. We need to understand what holds true right now. It takes courage and genuine curiosity to find out.

Because our beliefs and assumptions can be quite narrowing with respect to seeing the options available to us, it is important to broaden our perspective whenever we face difficult or changing situations. One way to broaden our perspective is to look at other people who have gotten through the same or a similar situation. This includes distant relatives, acquaintances, and public figures who have successfully overcome whatever we are going through. If someone has walked in our shoes, no matter how different they are from us, their life experience will offer us useful perspective on what is possible.

Sometimes this is hard for us to do. Even when we see an example of someone who successfully navigated a challenge or got their needs met in an exceptionally satisfying way, we might not relate. This is because we are taught to see differences between ourselves and other people. It does not matter if we perceive that the differences are good or bad—as long as they exist. We might believe that we are smarter / dumber than other people or more / less physically endowed. That alone can create the excuse to differentiate and isolate us when it comes to seeing our options. Suddenly, we are too different to fit in, find someone else who is like us, be judged fairly for who we are, etc. The only way to get past this obstacle is to realize that our beliefs that we are different from others are simply beliefs and nothing more.

Journaling / Meditation Questions

1. Think about a changing situation in your life. What is your reasoning with respect to your expectations and actions around it?

2. What beliefs and assumptions underlie your reasoning?

3. Write down what options you believe are inaccessible to you. Why do you believe they are inaccessible?

4. Can you think of someone who has successfully gone through something similar to what you are now facing? How did they handle it?

5. Do you believe you are different from other people in dealing with this situation? Why? What assumptions underlie that belief?

Chapter 5: Looking Beyond the Logic

We believe logic to be a superior decision-making tool in our professional lives and sometimes even in our personal lives. If someone challenges what we sense or feel with a logical argument, we are prone to cave in with respect to our position, disregarding our own good judgment. We do this because our senses and feelings are considered inferior to logic in our modern culture.

What we call "logical" decision-making usually has very little to do with logic, however. We as humans use a thin veil of logic to cover up our fears and flawed belief systems. We then use that veil to justify our decisions, claiming that they are "logical." Because we have such a strong cultural commitment to logic, most people will shut up and get out of our way when we lead with logic, even if our assumptions are problematic and our belief systems do not represent anyone's best interest.

We tend to shame people who do not subscribe to our particular form of logic by calling them irrational. For example, a corporate executive may announce that their company needs to make more money. They may then assert that extracting natural resources in a rural community will make money for the company. Their "logical" conclusion will be that the company needs to extract those natural resources in order to be profitable. Never mind that in the process they will destroy the local environment, community, and economy. Anyone who disagrees will be accused of being irrational for taking a position against making money. There are infinite ways of making money, and yet the corporate executive has silenced all other options by leveraging our collective cultural deference to logic.

Similarly, we shame ourselves using the logic that dominates our belief system. For example, an unemployed individual may desire to make money. The greater their fear that their financial needs will not be met, the stronger their commitment will be to pursuing financial security. As a result, they may take a job that puts their health in danger because it pays better than what they believe they could otherwise get. If any aspect of that individual objects to the idea of putting their health in danger, the part of them that is desperate for financial security will shame their health objection with the predominant logic that taking the job will make them more money. They may put up with the dangerous job in order to make money, even though there are better and safer options for them—ones they do not believe exist or are even available to them.

Our application of logic is straightforward at the surface but generally based on false beliefs and assumptions we have accepted as being true from our culture, clan, and individual experience. It is also based on our fears, which we also have internalized from the predominant culture in our world, as well as our negative life experiences. Fears that we will be lonely, poor, excluded, and so forth if we do not do X, Y, and Z. These fears only serve to corroborate our limited beliefs.

The author Andreas Moritz once wrote that "[a]ll beliefs contain their own intrinsic self-perpetuating system of logic and evidence. Each belief has its rationale, its relative truth and perspective....The basic principle here is that you will only be able to understand and create in your life what you believe is your truth. You see what you believe, not more, not less. There is no other reality out there than the one you create inside...." So be careful about being logical.

Our subjective logic is the tip of the iceberg of our shaky belief systems and emotional vulnerabilities. It is used to suppress the ideas and opinions of others and our better selves. It prevents us from facing our fears, thinking critically, being creative, and generally making progress in our lives. We become complicit to our adverse circumstances by buying into our self-limiting logic. And our personal logic becomes a tool of our own oppression.

Journaling / Meditation Questions

1. Think about a situation in your life involving change. Are there parts of you that want to be logical about it and others that feel or sense something different?

2. Have you shamed yourself for not following or not wanting to follow logical decision-making in the past? What did you ultimately decide to do? What was the outcome?

3. How have you shamed others for not following your logic? What beliefs and assumptions were the foundation of that logic?

Chapter 6: Getting Lost in Denial

Author Franz Kafka described our convoluted relationship to change in a short story entitled Metamorphosis. The main character wakes up one day to find out that he has turned into a cockroach. As he lies in bed having discovered his predicament, one of the first things he thinks about is how he is going to get himself to work on time and what his boss will think.

He does not wonder how it is that he turned into a cockroach. He does not view his former responsibilities as a person as wholly irrelevant to the current situation. Nor is he curious about his new body and the future ahead of him. Instead, he worries about fulfilling his obligations to his employer and the consequences of not doing so.

Each of us behave like Kafka's human turned into a cockroach with respect to change to some extent. We are resistant to recognizing emerging circumstances and the futility of continuing on our previous path. It does not matter if the changing circumstances are internal or external. Our initial response or behavior over the upcoming days, weeks, months, or even years will have some element of intellectual denial born out of emotional resistance.

This response is so predictable that it has been identified across the board in studies of human behavior —regardless of the type of change we face. We may lose a loved one, get divorced, quit our job, get dropped out of a plane, or get lost in the woods. It does not matter what specifically happens to us — it is enough that it disrupts our lives. We will all respond in a similar fashion to such change, although our perceptions and mental model will dictate how long into our changing circumstances our resistance to our circumstances will kick in, and how long it will endure.

The first thing to happen is that we will notice our reality deviates notably from our expectations. In response, we will feel disoriented or even lost. We will then enter a state of denial, where we avoid paying attention to evidence that all is not what it should be. We choose to believe at this point that our expectations are still accurate and not much has changed. Despite evidence to the contrary, we continue onward with our thought patterns for some time as though our original concept of reality still holds true, just like Franz Kafka's cockroach.

We fall into denial regarding a very specific aspect of change: the aspect that threatens the fulfillment of our needs. For example, a quarantine due to a pandemic will threaten our need to socialize and connect with others. A financial crisis will threaten our need for a dependable retirement fund. A rejection by a venture capitalist will threaten our need for financing. We may fall into denial regarding the nature of the threat because it is scary and painful for us to think about. We may also question the very existence of the problem in order to protect our perception of security surrounding our needs.

Denial of reality can turn to anger at the suggestion that something other than what we expect or believe is true. We may brusquely ignore or refute what others are telling us. We may lash out at anyone who claims that we should be expecting something different. We may conclude that people who think that anything has changed are crazy, overreacting, or untrustworthy.

We mostly think of denial in terms of a refusal to see that something negative is happening around us, but denial can also take the inverse form—that is, we can be in denial that what has or is happening around us is inherently positive. We may refuse to acknowledge the contributions of our colleagues, the positive intentions of our friends, the suitable life choices of our children, or the numerous opportunities we have available to us in any given situation.

On the other hand, we may also overestimate people and situations. We may entrust a project to a colleague because they make us laugh and feel good, completely overlooking the reality that they are unsuitable for the job. We may continue to make excuses for them while others complain about that person's performance.

Denial takes on at least three different embodiments, including denial of the past, denial of the present, and denial of the process of change. Denial of the past commonly occurs when individuals or institutions refuse to recognize former misdeeds. What can fuel this type of denial is our belief that a person is either good or bad. Admitting to these kinds of misdeeds in our culture would require us to conclude that we or others are bad people. Moreover, if we admitted to bad acts in the past, we would have to take on the burden of blame because our culture responds to misdeeds with social ostracism, punishment, and liability. Denial of the past is the reason we see so much anger and resistance toward victims in society. To accept their pain would be to accept the existence of events that would bring us pain and intellectual discomfort.

Denial of the present usually occurs when we refuse to see the gravity of a situation. Seeing things clearly would require us to take some responsibility in the matter to either course correct or embrace inevitable changes ahead. It would also unsettle us, triggering fears about the future. Our culture has conditioned us to fear and worry about the future a lot. Anything that disrupts our peace today is an unwelcome intrusion and threat to our future, rather than a positive invitation to change. As a result, we easily succumb to the denial of the present.

Denial around the process of change occurs when we refuse to acknowledge that our current approach to a situation is not working. It is one of the most common forms of denial. Every time we say to ourselves that something "shouldn't be happening," we are engaging in this form of denial. If something is happening, then it is not possible from the perspective of physics that it shouldn't be happening. It is happening, and we need to acknowledge its rightful place in current events.

Denial of the process of change can be a very complicated form of denial. It frequently occurs when people expect change to take a specific form and refuse to accept anything else. Take, for example, a person who continues to pursue someone romantically who is not interested in them rather trying to find someone else. Or a parent who wants their child to engage in something that is unsuitable for that child. Or an environmentalist who keeps lobbying an industry to become more sustainable with no success.

Denial happens because we build up expectations about how the world should work, how things should happen, and how other people should behave. When things do not meet our expectations, resistance kicks in —which is just another word for denial. We do everything we can to make the world conform to our grand plan. Sometimes this strong-arming works, but most of the time it does not. The world will simply not bend to our personal expectations.

If we are very attached to the outcome and believe our grand plan is the only way to get there, we will shift from denial to panic when things do not go as expected. Panic is a state in which we expend an enormous amount of energy in the wrong direction. The direction of our energy is wrong because we are still clinging on to our old belief system. We continue to pursue our original plan in some shape or form even more desperately, despite the evidence that it will not work. Many of us will get stuck in such a situation. Our misdirected energies will inevitably lead to unintended outcomes—missed opportunities, repeated mistakes, disrupted relationships, program failure, etc.

Journaling / Meditation Questions

1. Think of a situation that is not going your way. Identify the people and organizations that you disagree with.

2. For each such person or organization, list their position. This can be the opinions of your colleagues, acquaintances, the media, etc.

3. Is it possible that your perspective and the perspective of others can be true at the same time?

4. For each position that you disagree with, what would it mean to your life, your world view, and the fulfillment of your needs if you accepted their position as being true?

Chapter 7: Paying Attention

We model the world from the perspective of our physiological needs. This includes the need for tangibles such as food and shelter, but also intangibles such as love and acceptance. We focus our attention on information that we believe is relevant to the fulfillment of our needs. We categorize things as being good or bad based on whether we associate them with a positive or negative outcome with respect to getting our needs met. A smile on our mother's face, a smile on our boss' face. The look of discomfort in our spouse's eyes; the look of discomfort in our client's eyes. We perceive all of this information and build a mental model of it based on what we believe gets us closer or further away from the fulfillment of our needs.

Unfortunately, most of us are not very good at updating our mental model. By updating our mental model, I mean refining our understanding of the information coming in from the external world and its implications with respect to getting our needs met. We do this poorly in part because we simply do not pay attention very well to what is going on. We do not pay attention with our senses (which inform us about the state of the world) and we do not pay attention with our emotions (which inform us about whether we are closer or further away to getting our needs met). Both are critical for our wellbeing and ability to navigate a changing world effectively.

Indeed, our modern lifestyle discourages us from paying attention. We do a great deal of staring at our phones, computers, TV's and translating that information into thoughts. But we do a lot less of paying attention to the world around us. Even when we know we should be paying attention, we are out of habit. And so we filter out most of the external world. Our senses have become unduly skewed to hone in on digital communications as a source of our information at the expense of the inputs coming in from the rest of the world.

We also do not pay attention to what is going on inside of us. We ignore the fact that our hands have gotten cold, that we have gotten thirsty, that we need to use the bathroom, etc. We have become so bad at paying attention to our own physiology that we now rely on our devices to tell us when our blood sugar is low, how many steps we have taken, and whether we have been staring at the screen for too long. The end result of this is that we are not very aware of the physiological processes in our bodies and the physical indicators of whether we are meeting our basic needs.

We further do not pay attention to our emotions. Our emotions are our primary indicators as to whether we are getting closer or further away from getting our needs met. Most of us suppress our emotions, however. Frequently we suppress our emotions because they are painful and inconvenient—to us and other people. We are expected to buck up in our public lives, even when something terrible happens to us. If we lose a loved one, we are given a short grace period and then we are expected to get back to business. If we express fear or discomfort of any sort, we push it away, encouraged to be strong, courageous, positive, etc. This happens especially in our professional lives but it is also happening in our private lives.

Moreover, we tend to believe that the painful intensity of negative emotions will eat us alive. We believe that if we fully felt the anger we feel at our boss, we would be so consumed by it that we would have a heart attack or not be able to function. As a result, we stuff the anger down our throats and keep going. If we fully felt the sadness of a relationship break-up, we fear that we would just die or dissolve into a puddle of goo. And so we pretend it isn't all that bad. We stop paying attention to how we feel.

We also run clear of any negative emotions because we are afraid that we will react to them inappropriately. We think our anger would turn to rage and we would burn down the office or at least tell off our boss sufficiently that we would get fired. Or we fear that we will start crying during a business meeting and be totally humiliated.

Moreover, we have learned to mistrust our emotions because we all have had the experience of our emotional guidance system being wrong. Our mother-in-law criticized our actions and we overreacted, seeing it as a personal attack on our competency as a parent. We signed up for a time-share that we were so excited about during our vacation, and now we realize that we will rarely make use of it.

Because we are expected to have our emotions under control, we fear the consequences of feeling them. And because we have learned to mistrust our emotions they tend to be deeply underutilized as our resource. We stuff and suppress them, ignoring the signals they are sending us about the emerging events around us and their implications with respect to getting our needs met.

Because we are one step removed from our senses and emotions, we increasingly operate on autopilot within our existing mental model of the world, regardless of how faulty and flawed it may be. We simply do not update. New information is not getting in through our senses; and if it is, we refuse to digest or respond to it by suppressing our emotions. This makes us prone to denial of our changing circumstance.

Denial is essentially an interruption of the process of updating our mental model. We do not want to accept new information in front of us and so we don't. We shut down our senses and our emotions. As a result, we do not update our belief system and fail to adapt to our surroundings.

Journaling / Meditation Questions

1. How much time do you spend living in the present moment, versus the past or the future?

2. Do you pay attention to what is going on within your body? Why or why not?

3. Do you tend to notice the world around you? Why or why not?

4. Do you trust your emotions? Why or why not?

Chapter 8: Utilizing Our Senses

Our belief system is entirety reliant upon unimpeded communications between our senses, emotions, and thoughts in order to maintain up-to-date information about the world. As such, our senses and emotions must be fully operational in order for us to navigate new situations effectively. If any aspect of the communication process between our senses, emotions and thoughts is interrupted or not working properly, we do not make good decisions because we cannot fully digest new information and update our belief system to adapt to our environment.

We utilize our physical senses to explore the world and gather relevant information to getting our needs met. Our senses pick up on signals in our environment and give us feedback regarding how things are going. As a result of that feedback, we formulate emotions, which are positive or negative associations with any given set of circumstances. Our emotions are based on our cumulative experiences in life and our perspective on these experiences. Our emotional gauge of what is good and bad is subjective and is based on our personal preferences and belief systems, as well as the preferences and belief systems of others we have accepted as our own.

Our senses, on the other hand, are also our receptors for pleasure from the world around us. It is only to the extent our senses are working that we can experience the pleasure of a sunset view, the scent of flowers, the singing of birds, the taste of food, the touch of another, etc. The more receptive our senses become, the more pleasures we are able to experience.

Unfortunately in the modern world we frequently rely on cultural markers of success to generate pleasure (such as money, status, power, etc). Such cultural markers tend not to fully satisfy us because they are disassociated from the basic physical pleasures we are designed to experience utilizing our senses. By reactivating our senses we can naturally tap into pleasure, even when some of our needs and desires are not being fulfilled in this world.

The way we keep our senses working is by staying grounded in our bodies. Rather than living constantly in our heads thinking and obsessing about the thoughts of the day, we need to start living in our physical form. This means sinking into our physical being and cultivating a stream of awareness of what is going on inside of us and around us. The act of dropping into our bodies frees our minds from monopolizing emotional signals and repetitive thoughts that distract us from the here and now. Once we drop into our bodies, our sensory flood gates are able fly open and useful information can start to flow in.

I recommend you watch old clips of Arnold Schwarzenegger movies to understand the benefits of living in your body. Schwarzenegger consistently plays a character who is so grounded in his body that he is able to face most circumstances without flinching. He is not free of emotion and he certainly has his full intellectual faculties. However, his attention is attuned to his physical presence and the world around him, which helps him navigate danger. Not much gets past him. He is fully aware of his environment because he is fully present in it.

Schwarzenegger's characters are the type of people you would want to help you if you were trapped in a burning building because they would remain calm and find the exit. You want to assume the same physical presence as Schwarzenegger's characters—not to use force and violence in this world, as unfortunately many of his characters are scripted to do—but to navigate through life successfully.

In contrast, you need only watch old clips of Woody Allen movies to understand the consequences of living in your head, rather than your body. Although Woody Allen has an amazing ability to examine his thoughts and admit to his own emotions (which is a tremendous human asset), Woody Allen also generally personifies a neurotic personality in his movies. His characters are men who neglect their physical body and spend too much time exercising their brains. You will frequently find him tripping over something and being completely out to lunch with respect to the world around him. Woody Allen's characters are not the type of people you would want to resource if you were faced with a changing situation. They would go into paralysis trying to decide what to do if the building around them were to crumble, for example. Or fail to notice the exit sign in their attempts to escape because they would likely be lost in their head.

You may think you need to be living in your head in order to make the best decisions for yourself, but that is not the case. Your senses will naturally scan for relevant information from the external environment and your emotions will compare that data to what you already know. The very act of dropping into your body and allowing your physiology to resource the world around you will help you to trouble-shoot towards the best course of action without you having to consciously dictate the process with your mind. You are physiologically wired to do this in the same way you are physically wired to breathe, heal your own wounds, and digest your food. You do not need to force-think a solution or make any cognitive judgments when you are in your body. Your physiology will do it for you.

Journaling / Meditation Questions

1. Focus on your surroundings throughout the day. What do you see, smell, hear, feel, taste?

2. Pay attention to the physical sensations in your body throughout the day. Do you usually notice and respond to them? Why or why not?

3. When someone speaks to you about a subject matter you do not want to hear or talk about, what do you do? Do you pay attention and give them your time? Do you physically or intellectually run away from them?

Chapter 9: The Role of Emotions

Our emotions are repositories of our past experiences and are stored in our bodies. Many organs and systems are involved. Indeed, when we have an emotional response, we may feel sensations in our gut, chest, throat, etc. We may become physiologically cold or hot. Our blood pressure may go up or drop significantly.

Our bodies physiologically store, process, and communicate information through our emotions. These emotions become the foundation for enforcing our mental model. The next time we encounter a similar set of circumstances, our emotions fire, signaling to us whether the situation is good or bad. Our nervous system has many connections between various parts of the body and our brain to do this. These connections provide emotional feedback and wisdom from which we build our belief systems.

Our brain picks up on our emotional signals and translates them into thoughts. Emotional signals travel through a series of neural connections to our brain, telling us whether to see a situation in a positive or negative light. We then utilize those thoughts to either move toward or away from what we have encountered. We take action and move toward getting our needs met, wait where we are, or step back if needed. Then we get additional feedback based on the success of our actions. This feedback again takes the form of our emotions.

Our emotions may be accurate with respect to our past experience, but are not necessarily accurate with respect to the present or future. Each new event presents its own relevant set of circumstances. Our senses gauge to what extent our current circumstances reflect our past. Emotions regarding the past can be so strong, however, that they become overwhelming, drowning out the ability of our senses to do their job properly. We may stop receiving sensory input and instead get caught up in emotional signals before we have gathered all of the evidence. We jump the gun and our brain starts making decisions without having sufficient information.

Some people become so overwhelmed by their emotional signals that they begin to ignore their emotions. Ignoring our emotions, however, does not have the effect of freeing us from their grip. Rather, it moves these emotions into our subconscious, where they lay unresolved and dictate our behavior without much transparency. We are angry at our boss but we suppress the emotion; we then take our anger out on our loved ones or on strangers. We resign from our job after months of suppressing our frustration with the way things are run, while our boss is left to wonder why we quit.

Suppression of our emotions also causes us to ruminate in our heads. We have distanced ourselves from our physiological (i.e. emotional) response to a situation, but the feeling is still there, sending out signals to our brain. And so we keep thinking over about the same conversation—what someone said to us and what we should have said back. We also keep telling the same story over and over, without really ever resolving it in our minds.

Usually our rumination is linked to unresolved situations from the past that keep haunting us and are triggered by the most recent situation. These feelings refuse to go away because our brains are still ruled by strong undigested emotions from prior events that we never assimilated in our bodies, but rather ignored or suppressed.

Strong emotions call to us so emphatically because they need our attention. And that is what we are meant to give them. They want to be digested and processed through our biology so that they can properly be assimilated with our past experiences into our mental model of the world. If they do not get that attention, they will live as unassimilated fragments of memories. When these memory fragments get triggered, they will not come with the wisdom of the totality of our life experience. Rather, we are likely to have a strong response based on a past memory that is unsuitable to the present. And our emotions are likely to keep popping up, calling us toward resolution.

We have a tendency to keep trying to resolve these emotions with our brain because our modern culture has told us that the brain is for such purpose. But dealing with emotions is not the proper task of the brain. It is the proper task for the body. We can give our emotions our full attention by getting into our physical bodies to experience them viscerally.

To do that, we need to give these emotions our full visceral attention. This requires us to step right into the uncomfortable sensations our emotions create in our bodies. Physically experiencing our emotions allows our bodies to digest them in the same way our bodies might digest food: without intellectual effort on our part. Digesting these strong emotions so that they become properly assimilated into our mental model is critical for proper decision-making, especially when facing challenging or new circumstances.

The benefits of giving our emotions our full attention has been proven formally by researchers who studied a group of severely depressed people before and after treatment with psilocybin. Psilocybin is a psychedelic drug that occurs naturally in some mushrooms. It has the effect of temporarily setting our mental model aside, as well as the sensory filters and emotional suppression mechanisms we accumulate over time.

Before taking psilocybin, the depressed group of people reported being severely disconnected from their senses, including their sense of self, others, and their environment. They also had accumulated some fairly advanced habits and strategies in the practice of suppressing their emotions. Most of them also reported incessantly ruminating over the past and being imprisoned by their thoughts. These test subjects also described their depressed condition as an obstacle to making meaningful changes in their lives.

During treatment with psilocybin, the sensory and emotional floodgates of these patients were thrown open. They fully experienced the world around them through their senses and were able to directly face their darkest emotions. During and after psilocybin treatment, they reported being able to accept their negative emotions, where before they insisted upon repressing or running away from them. The treatment caused their emotions to swell to levels that overwhelmed their denial efforts; as a result, they were left with little choice but to surrender to them. Once they entered a state of surrender, their feelings would transform into useful cognitive insights or transition into more positive feelings. Moreover, these patients reported having the impression that their entire mental model of the world had been recalibrated.

You do not need to take psilocybin in order to recalibrate your mental model. But you do need to face your emotions and start living in your body, rather than your head. This practice will open up your senses, allow your emotions to flow through your physiology, and recalibrate your thoughts and belief system.

Journaling / Meditation Questions

1. Practice being present in your body on a daily basis
    —imagine that your mind actually sits within your
    body, rather than on top of it.

2. Think of a situation in your life that evokes a
    noticeable negative emotion within you. As you
    become aware of that emotion, drop your attention
    away from your mind and feel where that emotion
    resides in your physical body. It may be in your
    chest, your gut, your throat, or any other part of your
    body. How do you experience that emotion on a
    visceral level?

3. Send the feeling of love and empathy toward the
    negative emotion where you experience it in your
    physical body. Be present with it in the way you may
    be present with a loved one or a child who needs
    empathy and support. Imagine the negative
    emotion as a rolling wave (rather than a hard object)

and let its energy carry out its full course without trying to resist or manipulate it.

4. Think of a positive experience in your life. Let your body flood with the positive emotion the memory of this event evokes within you.

Chapter 10: Suppression & Trauma

Whenever we suppress our emotions in response to something, we risk creating trauma. We are used to thinking about trauma as something catastrophic that usually happens to people in their childhood. Rarely do we think of trauma as a frequent and regular occurrence that happens in adulthood to all of us. And yet this is the nature of everyday trauma in our modern world.

Trauma occurs when our nervous system gets into a fight/flight mode and we suppress our body's response to it. A threat jerks our nervous system into high gear and we are designed to actually physically flee or fight in response. The physical exertion of running away or wrestling with someone discharges the excess energy created by our nervous system in the case of danger. If we do not physically discharge that energy, we fragment the emotions associated with that threatening event and create trauma.

Depending on the context, severity, and length of a threatening situation, our nervous system may escalate from fight/flight into freeze mode. This may also occur when our fight/flight instinct is inhibited and we cannot leave a dangerous situation. Our bodies essentially shut down during freeze mode and are no longer able to respond to the potential danger. We can barely speak (if at all), we do not react any more, and we may not even be able to think clearly. Nevertheless, excess energy has still been created by the nervous system as it moved from its resting phase through fight/flight mode into freeze mode.

If we cannot fight or flee, our bodies are designed to physically shake off excess energy after danger has passed. When we shake we are physically sorting out the threatening experience and assimilating our emotional response to it into our existing mental model. If we do not have the opportunity to shake that energy off once we reach safety, we create trauma.

Our modern cultural tendency is to suppress our fight/ flight response, avoid conflict, and keep going. We rarely fight, flee, or shake in the modern world. Instead we suppress our feelings and visceral responses to our perceived threats. We also voluntarily subject ourselves to traumatic events every time we sign up for dental work, diagnostic procedures, surgery, expose ourselves to toxic chemicals, and subject ourselves to other situations to which our bodies would definitely say no.

These micro traumas distort our emotional body, our perceptions of the world, our decision-making capacities, and even our everyday responses to emerging situations. Traumas (even micro traumas) are one reason why people become unreceptive to opportunity and are unwilling or unable to navigate change. They see threats in situations others find to be relatively benign, and will resist progress.

Trauma leads to a state of fragmentation of our emotional memories. They are not integrated with the rest of our memories and life experience. They have a life of their own. Whenever an event triggers us, memories of the trauma come up but our brain does not understand that the circumstances have changed. It is dealing with the present as if it was a duplicate of the traumatizing event of the past.

When we linger on some past experience, dig in our heels, and tell others we don't want the current situation to end up like the past, we are likely dealing with trauma. When we overreact or under-react to a situation, we are also likely reliving trauma. When we ruminate in our heads, incessantly thinking about the same thing over and over, we are experiencing the aftermath of trauma.

Every society has social norms, economic structures and belief systems that can lead to trauma. For example, people who experience poverty in the US sometimes say that capitalism has traumatized them because they couldn't keep up paying their bills, even though they were working long hours at minimum wage. These are people who bought into the belief system that working hard in a capitalistic society will lead to financial freedom or security. They worked very hard but ended up struggling to survive. They blamed themselves and developed severe distress and trauma by staying within a work environment that wasn't supportive of them.

Further trauma has likely been layered on to their lives by others who regarded them as a failure for living in poverty and failing to succeed under capitalism. Nothing creates trauma like isolation and rejection by others because acceptance and belonging are part of our basic needs. When our needs go unfulfilled we feel threatened and our fight/flight response kicks in. If suppressed or unresolved, the isolation and rejection itself will create additional trauma.

We can release past traumas and recalibrate our nervous systems so that we are able to navigate the world successfully. Many chapters in this book are designed to do that, but here are some specific strategies to help release trauma. They can be used for current or past situations:

1. Engage physically with the excess or suppressed energy created when your nervous system went into fight/flight or freeze modes. Find a quiet place and give yourself the opportunity to shake it out, move your body, and make any sounds you want to make. This will not only help you release current excess energy but also help you release old trauma and integrate prior traumatic experiences.

2. Audit when your nervous system gets ramped up throughout the course of your week. Are there times when there is no immediate danger but you feel tense, alarmed, or ruminate excessively about things? Does this happen before, during, or after any set of circumstances? Do certain interactions other people trigger your response? Keep notes on what gets you

going and ask yourself what it would take to get you to let go of your alarmed response.

3. Reach out to other people and tell them what is going on with you. Look for moral and emotional support. Reach out to people you think have more wisdom than you, those with a different life perspective, and people who are likely to broaden your mental model of what is possible. Stay away from people who you think will narrow your perspective or focus your attention on your fears. It is important that you establish that you are part of a community, that you are safe in this world, and that you have support from others. Connecting with others for help and support is part of a healthy response to stress. Indeed, connection with others can prevent our nervous systems from entering into or getting stuck in fight/flight mode to begin with.

4. Focus your attention on how your emotions feel within your physical body. Sit with them. What

thoughts are coming up with these emotions? Be an independent observer of them. Send love and empathy to the areas of your body that feel frustrated emotionally and intellectually. Become aware of any patterns that emerge or any memories that come up. Frequently trauma is cumulative and a challenging situation today may be associated with a stressful situation from your past. Acknowledge the relationship between the past, present and how you think and feel.

5. Detoxify your body. Toxic chemicals can distort our thoughts and emotions. They do this by disrupting our hormones, undermining our nervous system, weakening our immune system, and by clogging up our organs and tissues in a way that prevents our bodies from being able to fully process our emotional experiences. To facilitate detoxification, choose natural clean products to put in, on, and around your body. Try gentle detoxification protocols to eliminate build-up of toxic chemicals in your system. And avoid substances that artificially alter the state of your mind or emotions if you

have the option to digest these emotions naturally instead.

The benefits of dealing with trauma—even adult micro traumas—are huge. We are better able to read the nuances of other people's facial expressions. We have better balance and physical coordination skills. We are more present in the moment, which means our senses are able to take in more information. We are more able to deal with physical tasks and challenges. We are more creative. And we are able to make better decisions for ourselves and those around us.

Journaling / Meditation Questions

1. Think of a difficult situation in your life. Did you fight, flee, or freeze?

2. Do you suppress yourself when potential conflicts come up?

3. Do you seek support from others when you feel threatened? Why or why not?

4. Think of a challenging circumstance in your life. Can you physically release some of your excess emotional energy around it through shaking, movement, dance, etc? Make sure you look out for your safety and remain present with your physical body and your surroundings at all times while you do this.

5. Are there specific circumstances that cause you to ruminate or cause your nervous system to become alarmed? Keep track of the frequency and context in which this happens. What would it take to get

you to let go of your alarmed response? Go back to the prior chapter and have an internal dialogue with yourself about the source of your alarmed response.

Chapter 11: Anger, Sadness & Fear

Any time our expectations are not met and we perceive that our needs are being threatened, we will experience anger, sadness, and fear. The relationship between anger, sadness, and fear is not necessarily linear. We may feel these emotions in any order and may bounce back and forth between them. Moreover, we are likely to feel one set of emotions around being a victim of a situation and another set of emotions around having to assume the responsibility for getting ourselves out of a situation.

Nevertheless, anger tend to hits us first when we are in denial or resistance. We are angry at the evidence that all is not what we think it is or want it to be—including the messengers of that evidence. Anger is a strong refusal to accept what we are seeing. We are outraged at something that has been said and done. We perceive that either it has directly interfered with our needs or threatens to interfere with them in some way.

The gravity of our anger is highly tied to our mental model of the world. The more committed we are to certain aspects of our belief system, the angrier we become when our expectations do not match reality. If we believe that A must occur before we can get B, then we will be outraged if A does not materialize. On a grander scale, if we believe that our happiness, security, belonging, or any other core value is dependent upon our job, reputation, health, or relationships, for example, then the potential loss of any of these will pull us into an emotional rollercoaster.

Some of us suppress anger because we have been taught that anger is socially inappropriate. In order to make this work, we may deny the existence of the changing situation or deny its emotional gravity in our lives. Suppression of anger, like with all emotions, causes us to have a distorted perception of the world. Suppression of anger results in a failure to recognize what forces are at play in creating or contributing to the circumstances around us.

When we suppress anger towards others, we frequently end up blaming ourselves when things go wrong—we conclude that we are not good enough, smart enough, communicative enough, etc. We blame ourselves possibly out of a fear of lashing out at others inappropriately or hurting them with our anger. Or because we have been taught that it is our exclusive responsibility to foresee and avoid the undesirable and unwanted elements in this world. This self-blaming strategy prevents us from fully recognizing the universe of forces at play that brought on and influence the situation.

Anger as an emotion can be an initial mask that shields us from other uncomfortable emotions. Indeed, accepting the existence of an undesirable situation would raise a whole host of other uncomfortable feelings—including sadness and fear about what is going on. As such, anger can become a tool for suppressing such other feelings.

Anger can be a very valuable emotion, however. It can be a powerful motivating force to the extent it gives us clarity regarding what needs of ours are not being met and what we want to have instead. With the clarity of what we need borne from anger, we can move toward positive action. We need not punish or lash out at anyone (or ourselves) with our anger. We can simply digest the emotion and utilize the feedback from what it is trying to tell us (i.e. that our needs are not being met or are threatened) to move forward toward meeting our needs.

Along with anger we will frequently feel fear. We fear that if things do not go as we expect then our plans will fall apart. We fear that our needs will not be met in the future—either by the options forced upon us by others or the road we believe we have to choose given our situation. We thus become resistant to the situation because we perceive the unwanted or unexpected is in direct conflict with getting our own needs met. We may start to behave obsessively, trying to control the actions, words, thoughts, or feelings of others. Our colleagues, neighbors, and family members become the obstacle to our perceived goals, success and happiness.

If we are our own source of the unwanted or unexpected behavior, we will try to control our own thoughts, feelings, words or actions. This frequently occurs when we believe we are not being productive, motivated, or agreeable enough, for example. We push ourselves harder to conform to our (and the world's) expectations, afraid of the consequences if we do not comply.

Fear is one of the most difficult human emotions. It is so uncomfortable that almost everyone tries to run away from it. Fear can also be paralyzing; we may become so focused on the fear of losing what we have that we cannot take any steps forward. Fear can easily shut down the senses and all other emotional responses if we give it too much bandwidth. As a result, it can also drive us to make poor decisions with little back-up information and out of sheer desperation.

Sometimes people will try to shame us into making choices based on our fears. "Shouldn't you be worried that..." they will say to us, suggesting that we are foolish for not following our fears. We may be tempted to give in to such suggestions, rationalizing that our lack of fear must be some form of intellectual denial. We are not in denial, however, simply because we choose not to make a fear-based decision. We may consciously choose not to give fear more weight in our decision-making process than it deserves. We can also consciously accept the potential risks of our actions. And if our worst fears come true, we can have the courage to live within that context.

Fear is a poor foundation for sound decision-making. It has been observed across many disciplines—such as psychology, philosophy and even foreign intelligence—that being in a state of fear leads to bad decisions, corruption, and nasty behavior. We tend to take more than our fair share when we are in a state of fear, sacrificing others in the wake. We also overreact and destroy things when we are in fear. Facing fear is thus critical for clarity of mind when it comes to facing changing circumstances.

We tend to fear taking action more than we fear the consequences of not taking action. That is why we frequently get stuck with the status quo. We may recognize that our current predicament is not good and that we are not heading in a positive direction. But our fear of speaking up or investing in another direction can be even greater. It has the mystique of the unknown—a void which we fill with fears laden with our assumptions and beliefs about the world.

Once we are able to face our fears and digest them fully, we begin to feel the sadness of our emerging situation. This can be the disappointment of knowing that our expectations of the world, ourselves, or others have not been met. Or the hurt and sense of loss associated with unwelcome change.

Sadness is painful and so we are habituated to suppress it so that we will not feel pain. Sadness, however, is also essential to recognizing that our needs are no longer being met so that we can recalibrate our mental model and pursue the fulfillment of our needs again. Feeling pain is necessary and essential for processing our sadness and getting beyond denial.

Our feelings of anger, sadness and fear all need to be faced fully by us before we can set our old mental model aside and move forward in the face of change. The way to face our feelings is to get inside of our body, be present with them fully, examine their validity, and thereby digest them, as discussed in the previous chapters.

Journaling / Meditation Questions

1. What angers you about the current or emerging situation and why? Sit with and feel your anger. Where does it reside in your body? How does that sensation feel?

2. What scares you about the current or emerging situation and why? Sit with and feel your fear. Where does it reside in your body? How does that sensation feel?

3. What would it mean if you accepted the current or emerging situation? Sit with and experience your sadness and pain. Where does it reside in your body? How does that sensation feel?

Chapter 12: Shame & Guilt

Shame and guilt are secondary emotions we feel in the process of change. They arise if what we are thinking, feeling, saying, doing or being is something other than what we believe we should think, feel, say, do or be. Our thoughts, feelings, words, and actions are a function of what is happening in our lives, our understanding of what is going on, our capacity to manage the situation, and our past experiences. Our reactions (or the reactions of others) may not be the collective ideal, but they do reflect where we (or others) are now.

Shame and guilt tend to push us away from seeing the world accurately because they cause us to focus on how we think that we, the world, and others in it should behave, rather than how we are actually behaving. However, asserting that someone (including yourself) should think, feel, say, or do anything other than what they are thinking, feeling, saying or doing now is beating our head against reality. Whatever is happening, is happening for some reason. By feeling that there is something wrong with us if we do not meet our expectations (or there is something wrong with others if they do not meet our expectations), we deny the reality of what is actually going on.

It is most helpful to understand the reasons behind our existing thoughts, feelings, words and actions (and those of others)—regardless of how inappropriate they may seem. They contain valuable information regarding the status of the world. Within them there is meaning and a message to us regarding what is happening and what needs to change. It is an opportunity to explore the motivations, emotions, beliefs, and assumptions that led to behaviors that are less than ideal.

We can learn the most from our thoughts, feelings, words, and actions if we are willing to look at our shame and guilt in the same way we would look at the face of our lover; with curiosity, love and our full attention.

Regardless of how ugly, unhelpful or inappropriate our thoughts, feelings, words and actions (or those of others) may feel to us. Berating ourselves for having them and pushing them away does not work. Embracing them and giving them our time and empathy does, however.

We sometimes do things that hurt others, inadvertently or intentionally. While at first blush it may seem that shame and guilt would be appropriate, they create problems in the long-run. We become stuck in our guilt and shame; they define our past and who we are in the present. They convert us into bad people when we are really human beings who made bad choices. And those choices were the best we could come up with at the time; otherwise we would have done better.

People also frequently feel guilt and shame around failure. This can be a business failure, a relationship failure, health failure, etc. Regardless of whether they also blame others, they frequently judge the outcome as being their own fault. They readily affirm this belief or it is readily affirmed for them by the successful people they see around them, the countless individuals who have never had to deal with the same situation, and extended family members who claim to know better. As a result, they are consumed with shame and guilt. They also lose faith in their decision-making abilities and become willing to convince themselves that others were right after all: they should have become an engineer, married that nice guy, done those juice cleanses, etc.

Shame and guilt undermine our faith in our own emotions and disrupt our self-confidence. They send us the message that where we are is not appropriate by society's standards. As a result, they separate us from everyone else and make us feel isolated. The only way we can become part of society again in a world of shame and guilt is to deny and suppress who we are, including what we think, feel, say, and/or do. Denying and suppressing ourselves only stunts our ability to process what is going on, grow, and flourish, however. We cannot function when we suppress our physiology.

Shame and guilt also put the needs and opinions of others first, which is problematic. Our entire physiology is calibrated to take care of our own needs first and foremost. Every living creature—from amoebas to fish to humans are designed to prioritize their own needs and opinions. This is a good thing. It is through prioritizing our own needs and opinions that we become strong enough—physically, emotionally, and intellectually—to help others. And yet, we are frequently willing to become powerless through the self-application of guilt and shame.

Journaling / Meditation Questions

1. Who do you think should be ashamed or feel guilty in the current situation?   Why?

2. How have others shamed you or made you feel guilty around the situation? What was your response?

3. Do you feel ashamed or guilty for any of your thoughts, feelings, words, or actions in the current situation? Why?

4. What would it feel like to accept your thoughts, feelings, words, or actions as having a purpose and message calling for change?

5. What would it feel like to accept the thoughts, feelings, words, or actions of others as having a purpose and message calling for change?

Chapter 13: Internal Conflict

We all have conflicting feelings in difficult situations because we have conflicting beliefs and assumptions about our role in society, how others will react to us, and how to best meet our needs. Our needs are frequently at apparent conflict with each other as well. We may have a desire to quit our job, for example, because it is not in alignment with our environmental values. This desire feels at odds with our desire for a stable salary and our need for security. We may feel conflicting pressures internally from all directions, in addition to any pressures from the world outside.

Rather than finding a solution that meets our divergent needs, we tend to succumb to our predominant logic. Usually this is the desire to protect our immediate safety —physical, emotional, or financial. We will prioritize this desire and reprioritize all others. For example, if your former boss fired you for expressing your feelings about the company's chemical safety policy, you may not express them in your next job. But your need and desire to stand up for yourself and others simply will not go away. It will inevitably still be there. As a result, you will have conflicting feelings between your concern about the company policy and your concern about keeping your job. Rather than becoming resigned and overwhelmed by such internal conflicts, it is better to acknowledge and resolve them. By doing so you will be able to come up with creative and alternative solutions to your problems.

American spiritual teacher Teal Swan points out that we have the capacity to have an internal dialogue between various aspects of ourselves and come to an agreement, in the same way we may work out agreements with others. This requires having a direct conversation with the aspects of ourselves that are for and against a given course of action. We need to understand the perspective of each aspect, including its underlying needs, beliefs, assumptions, fears, motivations, etc.

Fear is a frequent emotion that will drive one or more perspectives, and we come up with coping mechanisms in response to fear that are meant to protect us. However, fear is based on past events and circumstance. It does not necessarily have much to do with your current situation or it is usually only partially a legitimate concern. It will be your task to uncover to what extent your fear is warranted in the circumstances at hand, whether you can accept the consequences of what you fear and deal with them, and what you can do about reducing the risk of your fears taking place.

Have a dialogue with the aspect of yourself that feels fear and is trying to protect you. Start by identifying the needs of yours that seem in conflict given the current situation. For example, a part of you may have the need to speak up about something that is not right, and another part of you may feel the need to stay silent to protect you. Or there may be multiple parts of you with diverging opinions. Spend time identifying them; the following exercise will help you do that.

Write down what you wish to change in a given situation, what you consider doing to affect that change, and the fears you have about the outcome.

What I wish to change	
What I consider doing	
Fears about what will happen if I move forward	

Now write down your thoughts about this issue from the perspective of all of your various needs—regardless of how divergent they are from each other. I have outlined some of the core needs most human beings have for your consideration.

Your needs	Perspective from the aspect of you focused on this need
Safety / security	

Accomplishment of your goals	
Feeling in control of your life	
Feeling understood / accepted / like you belong	
Having autonomy as an individual	
Enjoyment of your life	
Making a positive impact on the world	

Look at the different perspectives that are originating from your needs. Do any of them seem like unsubstantiated beliefs, logical leaps, or invalidated assumptions about what is happening or will happen in your current situation? Identify where your beliefs are coming from. How can you validate them?

Assumptions or beliefs I hold about what will happen	
Where these assumptions / beliefs come from	
How reasonable are these beliefs?	
How can I verify my underlying assumptions?	

Think about what you consider doing given your situation. Is there a way to reduce the risk that one of your needs would suffer from moving forward?

What I consider doing given my situation	

The need that is at most risk from moving forward	
How I can reduce the risk of having this need suffer?	

Is there a way to approach the situation that would reconcile your conflicting needs?

My conflicting needs	
How to reconcile them	

Brainstorm alternative possibilities and futures you have not yet considered. For each one, consider how likely it is to take place. What beliefs and/or assumptions are hidden behind your conclusions?

Alternative possibilities / futures that I have not considered			
Likelihood of them taking place			
My assumptions / beliefs about how likely these futures are to occur			

Once you have had a chance to digest all of these thoughts, go back and reconsider how you might want to approach the situation.

Chapter 14: Getting Comfortable

We want to feel good, but in the absence of having our needs met, we tend to feel bad. Learning to feel comfortable in the present even when our needs are not being met is a critical skill because it calms our nervous system and allows our bodies and brains to work optimally. When we are comfortable we are better able to pay attention to opportunities, recognize which ones are suitable for us, and make good decisions for ourselves to find ways of fulfilling our needs.

Frequently one or more of our needs will not be met at any given time in this life. Nevertheless, we can still feel good in life while celebrating and pursuing our unfulfilled needs. One way to feel better is to feel appreciation for what we already have. Many times we do not even notice the things already available to us that are supportive of our needs. It can be the walk in the park we take whenever we want to relax. Or the friend who comes into our office regularly to help us blow off some steam. Learning to intentionally appreciate these things and mindfully feel the enjoyment we experience while tapping into these resources is a valuable thing. It transforms our daily life experience from one of lack to one of more happiness and fulfillment.

Another way we can feel better is by taking a few minutes on a regular basis to imagine our needs (as opposed to our desires) being fulfilled. This means experiencing on a visceral level how we expect to feel. How does safety and security feel in our gut, shoulders and back, for example? How does the sense of acceptance by and belonging to others feel in our heart, legs, and arms? This exercise is not about feeling the excitement of getting what we want or desire; this is about feeling the soul nourishing fulfillment in our muscles, organs and tissues of getting what we need.

This exercise requires an active intellectual acknowledgement that we are not presuming any specific route to fulfillment. Nor are we visualizing specific details of how our needs will be met and what the final outcome will look like. There are no parties we visualize attending, no awards we imagine receiving, no promotions we hope to get. Instead, we are simply focused on a sense of fulfillment. Lack of attachment to any specific path or outcome is critical. That way we stay open to opportunities that are not part of our grand plans.

The more we practice feeling the physical sensations of having our needs met, the more familiar we become with a positive physiological state of fulfillment. As a result, it becomes easier for our bodies, minds, and hearts to navigate toward the right outcome for ourselves. Rather than drifting further toward the negative state we are prone to become familiar with, we are able to swim toward the positive state we are training ourselves to recognize.

Spiritual practitioner Peter Fairfield describes the process of embracing a sense of fulfillment within our bodies as resembling the process of soaking up a dry sponge. At first we will wet a little bit of the outside or maybe one corner of the sponge, then the water will slowly soak in to the interior. Similarly, when we practice feeling a sense of fulfillment of our needs, we may viscerally feel emotions soaking into more and more parts of our body, like water. The more we practice, the more we can experience fulfillment throughout our entire body before we have even gotten our needs met. At that point we are tuned in to what we are looking for.

You may worry that by meditating on feeling good you may fall into a sense of denial regarding the undesirable around you. The pursuit of feeling good can become a form of denial when we suppress uncomfortable emotions as they arise in the present. Suppression can occur through meditation, so it is important to meditate on feeling good when other (i.e more negative) emotions are not calling for our attention. Moreover, we need to be conscious that human beings are good at suppressing or deadening their emotions with substances such as sugar, caffeine, alcohol, and many others. We also distract ourselves from our emotions with entertainment, our busyness, or by simply talking over our emotions—to others or in our own heads.

At the same time, we need to be careful about chronically feeling and being in a state of lack. Our bodies do not like it and do not operate well in a chronic state of stress. We also cultivate pent-up desires if we feel we are lacking too much because our physiology will start to desperately search for ways to fulfill our needs. The more pent-up our desires become, the more we will be prone to making poor decisions in trying to fulfill these desires. We will become less selective, stop tending to what we already have, and pursue things that are unsuitable for us.

We are good at pursuing things that are unsuitable for us because we think they will get us closer to what we need. For example, we may take a job, sign up for a class, or invest in a company because we believe it will result in us making money. We may not even like the things we sign up for but we do them anyway because we want to make money. While we are pursuing this goal we ignore the fact that we are trying to make money because it will help us meet some other needs. Instead of taking the indirect route, it is much more beneficial to take the direct route and focus on our true underlying needs and how to meet them doing things we enjoy.

Indeed, the things we enjoy are a reflection of what motivates us intrinsically and our intrinsic motivations are part of our internal navigation system. They will help lead us to the outcome we actually want.

We are also prone to taking on projects believing that we are doing it for one reason, while we really have ulterior motives we are not admitting even to ourselves. For example, we may start up a company, superficially telling ourselves that we are doing it to make money. Starting up a company, however, is not the most direct way of making money. If our true priority was to make money, we probably would never get involved in this type of enterprise because it is financially risky and requires a significant financial investment. Instead, we are likely to have other underlying needs that are motivating us. Identifying these priorities would help us think more clearly about our actions and pursue our life goals more effectively.

Understanding our needs directly will also help us communicate our needs and desires to others as well. This is important because the degree to which we are successful in meeting our needs is partially dependent on others. To the extent we can clearly articulate to them our true needs (Chapter 18), other people will have a better chance of actually helping us. If we obscure our needs, mislead others about our intentions, and pursue indirect goals because we think they will meet our needs, we are confusing other people and even potentially confusing ourselves.

Finally, it is useful on a regular basis to present the following question to ourselves (meaning, the totality of our internal navigation system, including our senses, emotions, thoughts and belief system): how can we get our needs met? We must do this without jumping into problem-solving mode or looking for an answer immediately thereafter. Instead, we need to let our subconscious physiology do the work. Essentially we are placing a request upon our internal navigation system to pay specific attention to opportunities that will be helpful to us. In order to do that, we need to understand what needs we are trying to fulfill. Do we want to feel safe and secure? Loved and accepted? Like we've accomplished something meaningful? Understanding must come before all else.

Journaling / Meditation Questions

1. What are your needs and desires in the current situation?

2. Are your needs and desires direct or indirect— meaning, are there other motivations hidden behind them?

3. If your needs were met how would you feel? Safe? Accepted? More autonomous? Can you practice feeling those emotions now in your body?

4. Sit with the feeling of fulfillment in your heart. Ask yourself how you can get to that destination and remain open to what routes you can take along your journey.

5. What resources do you already have that are supportive of your needs? Can you mindfully enjoy having and experiencing them?

Chapter 15: Cultivating Acceptance

We get tied to how things should happen, in what way, and when. Anything presented to us outside of that realm will usually trigger denial. We push and pull away in an attempt to make the undesirable or unexpected go away. We resist moving toward acceptance of the situation as it really is because it takes us on a path of uncomfortable emotions. We feel uncomfortable with the idea that something will be or has been taken away from us. More specifically, that our needs will not be met.

We cannot comprehend a situation if we are busy pushing or pulling away from it. We have to accept reality in order to create the mental space to understand and navigate it successfully. If we do not fully understand a situation, we will put our energies into efforts that do not actually help us make any progress. We will beat our heads against brick walls pursuing the wrong thing, generate conflict in our relationships due to misunderstandings, make rash decisions with insufficient information, become paralyzed with fear, lash out at others in anger, etc.

Frequently we employ denial toward our own selves, which severely clouds our judgment and decision-making. We deny our own feelings, thoughts, and needs if they are not in alignment with our expectations of what our feelings, thoughts, and needs should be. Our expectations of how we should behave are based on our mental model or belief system. If we do not conform to those expectations, we are prone to shame, blame, judge, and berate ourselves. As a result, we suppress our thoughts and feelings and/or actively resist them.

Our resistance to our own thoughts, feelings, and needs hugely undermines our ability to navigate the world. Recall the group of severely depressed patients from Chapter 9 who suppressed their emotions on a regular basis. These patients described their depression as an obstacle to making meaningful changes in their lives. During and after treatment, these patients reported being able to accept their negative emotions, where before they insisted upon repressing or running away from them. Once they entered a state of acceptance, their feelings would transform into useful cognitive insights. Negative feelings would also diminish or dissipate. As did their depression and their self-reported inability to navigate their world.

Acceptance must come before any attempts to change anything because usually we are trying to change the wrong thing, anyway. We need to let go of what we have been doing or clinging on to that does not hold true and/or does not work so that we can focus our energies into a potentially more effective direction. We stop pursuing the job that does not suit us, stop trying to change our spouse, and stop trying to change dysfunctional institutions that do not want to change. We instead sit still long enough to see that our energies can be better served invested into something else.

Acceptance means to embrace something as it is, without trying to deny its existence, run away from it, or change it. It is synonymous with bringing love, patience, attention, and appreciation for our surroundings, ourselves, and the people in it. It also means getting comfortable with where we are now, even if our worst fears have come true. It is only in becoming comfortable with our reality—regardless of how much it terrifies us—that we can be open to better options going forward, including possibilities we never conceived are even possible.

To take a step even further, acceptance means having fun with where you are now. The challenges in front of you are an adventure, where you appreciate the experiences long the way. You stop focusing on the threats that changing events can create with respect to the fulfillment of your needs. Rather, your focus is on pursuing your needs through curiosity and playful discovery. The curiosity and exploration born from acceptance creates room for us to take in new information for the purpose of figuring out how to best meet our needs and accomplish our goals. Our capacity for problem-solving and creativity increases exponentially. We are no longer in denial of the reality around us, no longer in resistance to what is happening, and no longer trying to change and manipulate the people around us to fit our mental model. Instead, we take the world as given and get to the business of exploring that reality.

We also realize over time that we can still experience happiness without one or more of the things we expected. Once that realization comes and we are able to embrace it, we suddenly develop the capacity to regain what we have lost, although in potentially much different and more meaningful ways than ever before. We create new and even better circumstances with respect to our careers, relationships, health, community, etc. In short, we grow and develop as human beings through the process of change and emotional acceptance.

You may have taken a yoga class before. When you stretch your body into the downward dog position, your yoga instructor will frequently tell you to get comfortable. Initially you are huffing and puffing and feeling out of sorts. Over time, you learn to relax and sink into the pose. It's really not that bad, you realize, and it becomes possible for you to stay in that position much longer. That is what you are doing when you get comfortable in a potentially adverse situation. You are getting comfortable; and as you do, you learn to accept where you are now, thereby broadening your intellectual capacity to navigate challenging and emerging conditions.

Many people are unwilling to accept a situation because they believe acceptance means approval. To approve of something means to believe that it is good or desirable. To accept something, on the other hand, means to embrace its existence in our lives as it is—including all of its benefits and disadvantages, constraints and opportunities, ugliness and beauty. Acceptance gives us the capacity to see clearly what is going on around us so that we can adapt to a situation. This does not mean becoming resigned to a situation or conforming to it. It means updating our belief system to reflect current reality so that we can successfully navigate that reality.

Acceptance has been studied in the context of wilderness survivors and people grieving a significant loss in their lives; the experience of these individuals is instructive for the rest of us. People who survived getting trapped in an avalanche or who broke a leg hiking alone in the middle of nowhere have especially proven the value of acceptance. These survivors cultivated an exceptional acceptance of the world around them before they could effectively deal with their crisis.

After initial rounds of denial, anger, fear, and panic, they reported calming down and accepting their situation. They describe entering almost a spiritual state of love and attention for their immediate surroundings, appreciating the beauty around them fully with their senses. This state of mindfulness made it possible for them to become clear-headed and problem-solve. Those who panicked or refused to accept their surroundings perished—even if they had several days' worth of supplies and were just a few miles from civilization.

A similar state of acceptance has also been reported in terminally ill cancer patients administered psilocybin for grief management. They found not only that they were able to accept their situation, but they were also able to accept other situations in life, including the "flaws" they saw in other people. Their relationships improved, their levels of happiness improved, and they were no longer terrified of dying. Nothing had changed in their reality —they were still terminally ill with cancer. The only thing that changed was that they were no longer resistant to and in a panic about their situation. Their state of acceptance endowed them with the physical,

mental, and emotional bandwidth to enjoy their lives—
even more so than they had ever done before.

Journaling / Meditation Questions

1. What is most uncomfortable about the situation you are in now and why? Can you spend time feeling that discomfort on a visceral level?

2. What would it mean to accept the current reality and let go of your expectations? What would be the consequences of that and how could you live with them?

3. If you could not change the current situation at all, how would you think, feel, speak, and act differently? What different choices would you make?

Chapter 16: Managing Perfectionism

We navigate our lives utilizing our internal navigation system. This includes the details of our relationships, career choices, hobbies, etc. We are so attached to the various outcomes of these projects that we become terrified of failure. Whether it is planning an event, a life transition, or beginning a new task at work, we can become vulnerable to perfection in our attempts to avoid failure. As a result, we can hijack and paralyze our journey with the pressure to get it right.

Not all of us are terrified by failure equally and in the same circumstances. Some people were told growing up that they are prone to certain types of failure, and have internalized that criticism as an immutable truth. People who did well in school are also particularly vulnerable to failure because they take it personally. Our educational system is set up around grade performance, where failure defines capacity. Those that did well in school usually have internalized the belief that capacity is fixed, and they happen to be well endowed. A subsequent failure in adulthood has an awful meaning to them: that they must have a limited capacity for success after all. In reality, our capacities are constantly evolving.

Indeed, failure is part of the evolutionary process. Every organism explores the world with a certain amount of trial and error. Octopus as a species are some of the most extreme examples of this, as they usually grow up without the presence of any adult caregiver and learn about the world entirely from their own personal explorations. They try new things and change course depending on how things go. They learn that different strategies work in different situations. And some strategies do not work at all. Each success and failure provides an additional piece of information for their own personal evolution. The same truth applies to us.

We have the capacity to learn from trial and error and evolve. Moreover, the world is constantly changing and demands evolution from us. We may accept this idea in theory, but nevertheless we convince ourselves that we can successfully plan out our creative life projects from start to finish as well as their outcomes. We then obsess with trying to predict whether they will be successful based on our progress before there is enough information to make that decision. If things are not going as planned along the way, we believe that we have failed.

By definition when we start on any journey and before we are done we will have insufficient insights and information to get to the finish line. Those will develop along the way, and this will require some trial and error. We may have a clear vision or expectation of what we are about to do, but we need to be able to set that aside from moment to moment and just move forward with whatever comes our way. This includes things thrown at us from the external world as well as things that come out of us in terms of ideas, designs, etc. We need to just humor ourselves and keep going.

This is the creative process. It is not bound by precise plans, judgments, and expectations. It is open-minded, full of curiosity, and is the critical part of our successful evolution. If we are willing to let go of our expectations enough, it will also be fun and create a state of flow within us. That flow can only come if we do not summarily cut off our stream of creativity because we disagree with the direction and type of flow we are getting.

The worst disasters happen if we try to censor ourselves or others. We tend to do that a lot. We are usually unwilling to let out bad ideas and ugly designs into the light of day because they threaten our self concept. We believe that what is being generated is not good enough and we erroneously believe it reflects poorly on our abilities or threatens us as the decision-maker. We then become paralyzed throughout the journey by our fear of failure. As a result, we suppress creation before anything worth developing has come out.

We need to set our expectations aside and instead focus on finding the path of open-mindedness and enjoyment with each step we take. If we choose to follow this route, we will develop solutions that are much better than we ever imagined. We will gain new insights and new perspectives along the way but the road will rarely go in the direction we or others have planned.

Journaling / Meditation Questions

1. What happens when things are not going as you
    expected? What do you do? What do you say?
    What goes through your mind?

2. How do you censor yourself?

3. How do you censor others?

4. How would it feel to take baby steps without trying
    to predict your path to the final outcome?

Chapter 17: Beyond Productivity

Another common challenge to our internal navigation system is our relationship with productivity. We are elated when we get things done. We feel important, successful, and optimistic. When we are not making as much headway as we think we should, things look a lot differently. We get scared and anxious that we will not make our deadline. We might even become terrified that we will not be able to reach the finish line at all. We may even become paralyzed and hijacked by fear.

When we exhaust our productive capacities, our bodies tend to fall into a listless daze. At first, we think this is okay. As more time passes, however, we start to judge ourselves for not having accomplished anything. Because we do not feel comfortable with such longer periods of time being unproductive, we reach out for coffee, tea, chocolate, cheesy poofs, alcohol, cigarettes, and/or a myriad of other substances that give us that boost we think we need to get back on track. We do this because we have a very strict cultural understanding of productivity: that we must consistently produce as much as possible per unit of time and on demand.

Few of us know that our concept of productivity has its roots in colonialism and slavery. American cotton mills had a huge interest in having African slaves produce as much cotton as possible. As such, they came up with accounting and management systems to help the wealthy land owners maximize the productivity of their slaves—that is, the slave's output per hour, day, week, etc.

You can probably imagine the sordid details involved in the process of keeping enslaved individuals working as much as possible. Slaves were expected to be physical production machines. They were not asked their opinion. They were not called upon for their creativity. Nor their ability to innovate or problem solve. Rather, they were there to pick cotton—as much cotton as possible.

The accounting and management system that grew out of the slave trade was eventually embraced by corporate America. Originally workers on the assembly line were tracked for their productivity. Eventually even professional white collar workers became judged by how consistently productive they were. Unfortunately productivity does not equal creativity nor does it guarantee success.

Creativity and problem-solving require a lot of back-processing that only occurs during times when we are not working. These are times when we are playing, noodling with something, taking a walk, sleeping, etc. Even those down times when we are feeling listless and are doing nothing at all are essential. They are an indicator that our brains and bodies are taking a much needed break to recharge.

When we are faced with a new situation or task, our subconscious mind is being challenged to learn. And learning takes time. New associations have to be built.

Thoughts and ideas, like jig-saw puzzle pieces, must be tried and tested as associations in the realm of our subconscious until they fit with the totality of our life experiences in some satisfactory way. This learning can only take place if our conscious minds are taking a rest break and not obsessing about the problem. In other words, our conscious minds need to get out of the way.

The body tells us it is time to take a creative break when we lose momentum. Often times we will simply lose motivation to move forward. We may also feel foggy brained, bleary eyed, tired, or generally spacey. This is our internal navigation system telling us to stop what we are doing immediately and take a break. We need to reconfigure.

Motivation is our compass for whether we are headed in the right direction. If we lose motivation, it is time to stop until we pick it up again. That is the golden rule. Do not force yourself, or else your efforts will suffer. When you lose motivation, it is not the time to drink another cup of coffee, shove a cookie in your mouth, or do any of the other things that you do to strong-arm yourself to keep going. You are at the cross-roads and whether you realize it or not, you need to make some complex decisions on the subconscious level before you move forward. You will be tempted to move forward because you want to be productive. However, chances are high that you will be wasting your energies on the wrong thing and getting even more deeply committed to a misleading path.

What if nothing comes to you? Well, you will just have to wait. How long? Until you are genuinely motivated to work on the problem again. Go work on something else, go play, get some exercise, or simply take a break. And do not think about the problem. Worrying about when your motivation may return will only drain your creative energy. It is sort of like opening the oven when the soufflé is not ready. It will deflate you and set you back further.

Your focus could instead go toward relaxation and becoming free of the pressure you are putting on yourself. That pressure can be around perfection (and failure—its counterpart) or productivity. If you move forward with a project with any one of those self-imposed pressures, it will lead to creative blocks. And it will prevent you from seeing opportunity. The old saying is that when one door closes another opens. However, you will not even see the door of opportunity if you are too worried about being productive to do so.

Sometimes we lose motivation because we subconsciously feel fear, anger, sadness or other emotions related to our path forward. These emotions can become a creative block, taking the wind out of our motivational sails. We need to face these emotions fully before we can move forward. We can do that by asking ourselves why we have lost our motivation to move forward and having an internal dialogue with ourselves about the matter (as discussed in Chapter 13). Frequently, however, it is enough that we simply indulge in our state of listlessness to its fullest and pay attention to any feelings that may come up when we allow ourselves to completely relax.

Journaling / Meditation Questions

1. What do you think and feel when you are not productive?

2. What do you say to yourself and others when you are not productive?

3. What do you do when you are not productive?

4. Can you sit with the physical and emotional discomfort of not being productive and accept this state of being?

5. What do you fear most about not being productive?

Chapter 18: Working With Others

People either meet or do not meet our expectations in the same way that our circumstances either meet or do not meet our expectations. When people do not meet our expectations, we tend to get angry, sad, and fearful. This is because our expectations are part of our grand plans for how things should move forward in our lives, or in this world in general. If someone does not meet our expectations, they are disrupting our grand plans. And we view disruptions of our grand plans as threats to meeting our goals and living happy lives.

We can go into denial when someone does not meet our expectations. We may simply ignore the person or their behavior, denying that aspect of reality. Or we may resist that a person's behavior "should" be happening, criticizing them to their face or to others in an attempt to get them in line with our agenda. If we ignore their behavior it is usually because we want to avoid conflict with them. If we resist their behavior, it is because we believe conflict and pressure will get them to meet our needs.

Between staying silent and criticizing others exists at least one other option. That option is to articulate to others what we ultimately need, and what we desire from them specifically. That requires some forethought on our part. We first need to identify our own needs, feelings, and desires. We also need to be able to identify the reasons behind our needs, feelings, and desires, as well as our beliefs and assumptions underlying them. We must become conscious of all of this for ourselves before we can get into a meaningful discussion with anyone else.

Communication also does not work if we approach others with the perspective that we are right and they are wrong. Rather, we need to understand that the way we feel about others is a function of whether they are meeting our needs and expectations. Whether people meet our expectations are cultural and subcultural constructs that are subjective to each of us. Whether people meet our needs and desires is also subjective. For example: a bad employee in your eyes can be a good employee in someone else's eyes. And a terrible boss in your eyes can be a very good boss in someone else's eyes.

Most people have no idea what impact they have upon our needs and desires. They need to hear from us—not about what they are doing wrong but what words or actions we desire from them specifically. The art of asking for what we desire from other people in order to help meet our needs is covered extensively in the workshops and books by Marshall Rosenberg, who teaches a communication style that is designed to help us communicate our needs to others and understand the needs of others. It is a difficult style to master, however, and requires inner peace from us first.

To obtain that inner peace, we need to think about and understand how we ourselves feel in a given situation.

We then need to figure out what we need for ourselves. Finally, we need to figure out what specifically we desire from others in order to help meet our needs. Once we know what we need and desire, the best we can do is express that to other people, without criticizing them for not meeting our needs, desires, or expectations. Maybe our needs and desires can be met by the person in front of us, maybe not. If not, chances are very high that another human being can do so, given that there are billions of us on this planet.

We tend to think that if someone is not meeting our needs and desires then they are bad. If they are meeting our needs and desires, they are good. The world is not so simple, unfortunately. How we feel about other people is subjective. We are not necessarily right and other people are not necessarily wrong. There is also not one single appropriate way of behaving in a situation, although each of us has our own ideas of what we expect.

Unfortunately, in our society it is common for people to criticize others in an attempt to meet their own needs. We realize that criticism leads to conflict, but we struggle to ask for what we need in a more benign manner. As a result, we avoid friction by staying away from potentially uncomfortable topics. We engage in self-censorship when we do not want to alienate other people, offend them, or get an aggressive response in return. We also engage in avoidance, skirting the issues, false flattery, and manipulating the truth in order to avoid friction.

When we suppress asserting our needs this way, we significantly reduce the chances that our needs will be met. We may also be traumatizing ourselves by not responding to our internal fight, flight, or freeze signals with respect to what others are doing or saying to us (refer to Chapter 10 on trauma). We also sometimes stop making decisions based on what we need, but rather, based upon our projection of how we think others will perceive our words and actions.

We usually assume how others will react based on some experiences from the past that are not necessarily applicable to the present. Or we may assume what others will think without actually talking to them, thereby limiting the possibilities for how to go forward. This is frequently used to dismiss opportunities available to us, by assuming that our boss, spouse, or anyone else who we think needs to agree with us will never do so.

Moreover, we sometimes agree to do things in order to please other people and gain their approval. Both are very dangerous games to play. We frequently get caught in trying to please everybody (which is impossible), by offending nobody (which is also impossible). The only thing we successfully do by this strategy is we lose track of ourselves and suppress our own needs. We also lose our own good judgment in the process.

Journaling / Meditation Questions

1. Think of an important situation in your life where you stayed silent, even though you also felt the desire to speak up. What emotions did you feel at the time?

2. What were your needs and how could you have stated your needs without criticizing the other person or parties involved?

3. Think of a time when you made a decision not based on what you wanted but your perception of what someone else would think, feel, say or do. Did you specifically ask that person for their actual perspective? Why or why not?

4. Think of a situation in your life currently that requires you to navigate an undesirable or unexpected situation. Describe the ways in which your assessment of others in your current situation is subjective.

Chapter 19: Understanding Others

Other people have to go through the same internal process that we do in order to navigate the world successfully. They must be able to accept the nature of their problems and take personal responsibility for moving toward a solution. This means they will have to deal with their own internal denial—including their outdated mental model, false assumptions, and threatening emotions such as anger, fear, and pain. This is not something we can do for them. It is part of their journey of self-discovery and discovery about the world.

Unfortunately we are prone to thinking we know better than other people and want to take over their internal navigation process. We can be supportive of their journey, but we are not a substitute for it. Moreover, unless we understand other people's internal challenges, their needs, and beliefs, we cannot have a positive influence on them. We can be supportive of other people by listening to their internal dialogue. We can ask them questions about their beliefs, assumptions, feelings, etc. We can also utilize our senses to become aware of their body language and responses while they speak. This becomes easier for us to do the more we become intimately familiar with our own internal navigation system and our own intellectual, sensory, and emotional journey.

But we need to be careful about drawing assumptions about what other people are thinking, perceiving, feeling, or needing. Instead, we need to ask for clarification or more information before jumping to conclusions. Only once we have gathered such information does it usually make sense to offer other people our own perspective or advice. If we think we truly have valuable information for them we need to ask them whether they have considered such information already (rather than assuming they have not). They may explain why they have rejected that information and thereby give us more insight about their perceptions and reality.

In listening to other people, we may learn that we were not as clear about things as we thought we were. Indeed, many times we think we understand our (or other people's) problems, but we do not. As a result, we go about solving the wrong problem and put our energies into the wrong direction. This is because when we fail to listen to other people we are actually in resistance to and in denial of their reality. Moreover, if we have not accepted other people for where they are then we have not truly accepted our own reality because they are a part of it.

A great example of this is found in a case study presented by IDEO, a design company known to interview potential customers before designing products for them. One of their clients asked IDEO to design a software tool that would teach low-income individuals how to manage their money. The client's assumption was that low-income people do not know how to manage their money, which leads to financial crises. IDEO reached out to this low-income demographic and learned that they were actually quite good at managing their money. IDEO also learned that what actually causes this low-income demographic to spiral into financial crises are unexpected events such as acute health problems, car troubles, etc. These events require more financial resources than these individuals normally have.

Similarly we need to listen to other people so that we understand their world (and our own) more accurately. The key to listening is to be committed to setting aside our own perspective for an hour or two and to be willing to give others our full attention. Instead of interjecting our own thoughts, perceptions, and opinions, we need to be fully present with theirs. Being present with them means to fully embrace and accept their reality to the degree that we can experience a state of wonder and appreciation for what they have to tell us about their thoughts, beliefs, emotions, and sensory experiences. This is the same state of wonder reported by wilderness survivors (as discussed in Chapter 15) who were able to focus their attention and appreciation for the world around them, and thereby accept and get comfortable in their reality.

Many problems in this world exist because people's need to be understood and accepted is not being met. We are not understanding or accepting if we are in resistance to other people, assume we know better than them, and talk over them to get our own perspective heard. This only pushes other people away from us because we are undermining their fundamental need to be understood and accepted. Conversely, it is very difficult to get our own needs met from someone else who is unwilling to understand and accept us. Misunderstanding and lack of acceptance create emotional alienation that lead to social division and the inability to problem solve—individually and collectively.

Journaling and Meditation Questions

1. Describe a situation in which you have tried to get other people to change their thoughts, feelings, beliefs, words, and/or actions unsuccessfully.

2. Do you think you know better than other people when it comes to understanding certain problems or developing solutions? In what ways might they know more than you?

3. In the context of your situation, ask others about their needs, problems, and perspective without attempting to impose your own needs, problems, perspective and solutions upon them.

4. Can you set aside your perspective and develop a sense of wonder and appreciation for theirs?

Chapter 20: The World's Problems

Collectively we steer the ship in the direction we are heading. And each individual is contributing to the direction with his or her own personal mindset. Through no fault of our own, our mindsets are aligned toward the status quo. We may have every intention to create or embrace change, but our mindset is not fully on board with this. We have a stake in the game with the respect to the status quo, and that keeps us anchored. The stake does not need to be obvious or financial. It can be much more subtle, and be chained to how we feel about ourselves, our relationship to others, and about various aspects of change.

As a result, each of us will have a hard time accepting that a problem exists with respect to some issue in this world. We will be so vested in our belief system that revising it will be highly uncomfortable. It would mean accepting that we have been duped into a lifestyle that is not in our best interest or that is contributing to the problem, for example.

Sometimes we are willing to intellectually comprehend that a problem in society exists, but we also convince ourselves intellectually that a solution is not warranted because the impact of the problem is not significant enough. Usually we utilize misunderstood and partially true principles to justify our reasoning and avoid facing the issue.

Many of us will understand that a problem exists, but will not understand its true nature. We frequently see only the outcomes of a problem, such as people's angry responses to it, and mistake the outcomes for the source. Usually we are in denial about the problem's true source because we do not understand what triggered the reactions of other people. We are also frequently complicit in the problem—not because we intend to be but because we follow the rules of a society that has set up the dysfunctional situation to begin with. Indeed, further investigation of the problem might will lead right back to us—including the social and economic dynamics we support with our habituated belief systems, thoughts, feelings, words, and actions.

Some of us will accurately acknowledge the existence of some of society's problems. This might lead us to feel anger at the situation, but not necessarily a sense of personal responsibility to do anything about it. Instead we may initially assign blame and responsibility to other people. That is, we demand that others come up with the ultimate solution and disassociate from our own role and responsibility as citizens.

Fear is the number one reason why people fail to take responsibility for helping solve our world's problems. We feel insecure about speaking out and/or taking action when we know we should. We worry about what other people think and we also fear the risks of moving forward, including the social, financial and legal uncertainty it will bring. The more we give in to our fears, the more we feel powerless to do anything about our problems. We justify not taking any steps at all. We may then revert back to blaming others about the problem so that we don't have to deal with our fears. Facing fear and other difficult emotions is key to taking responsibility for what we can do in the present moment to move toward getting our individual and collective needs met.

Another general reason why we do not take more responsibility is because culturally we associate the act of taking responsibility with culpability or liability for a problem. No one wants to take on culpability or liability; it just does not feel good. Culpability and liability leave us socially isolated from others and burdened financially and emotionally by the adverse consequences of our individual and collective actions. What we really want instead is understanding, support, and acceptance.

We are conditioned to point the finger at other people, the government, corporations, and others for problems in order to avoid culpability and liability. Such blame does not lead to change. It only causes people to clamp up and resist change even more. No one wants to be a bad person or be isolated from others by being labeled culpable. Indeed, none of us are bad people; we are simply people who sometimes do bad things. And the bad things we do are never done in isolation. They are influenced by the actions and pressures from others living on this planet.

Many of us will feel the pain of living in an imperfect and sometimes dysfunctional culture. This will especially be the case if we feel ready to take action but others are not. The more we try to move them along toward change, the more they will resist us. Indeed, we will become a source of discomfort, fear, and trouble for them. They may exclude us from their clan and even become hostile toward us. The more we try to bring them along on our journey, the more resistance we will get from them.

This separateness will feel extremely painful and overwhelming to us. As a result, we may experience a sense of being underutilized in society, a sense of loneliness in our purpose, and even a senselessness about our world. When this happens to us, we need to refocus our energies on digesting our pain, anger, and fear around our frustrations. In surrendering to these emotions we process our adverse experience so that we can learn from it and be inspired to choose our next steps, better informed about the world.

No single individual is responsible for solving the world's problems. Our lives are interrelated and we are dependent upon one another. Each individual is just one of many forces at play that will influence the nature of the solution. Indeed, each of us has our own sphere of influence or responsibility in this world. This includes what we choose to believe, think, feel, say and do. At the very basic level, we must each consciously choose to pursue our own needs, utilize our senses, embrace our emotions, seek to understand others and regularly update our mental model.

By focusing our energies on doing this — and by taking baby steps from moment to moment toward these goals — we will start to see other opportunities for how to influence and create change within ourselves and others. If we instead operate out of fear, unvalidated assumptions, and a narrow-minded mental model of the world that is out of touch with reality, we will contribute to poor decision-making in our lives and society in general.

No matter how broad-minded and enlightened we become, we cannot predict how the world's problems will be solved. Each of us, however, can take responsibility for the choices we make in any given moment. We can pursue our needs directly, seek to understand the needs of others, face our fears and other emotions, and accept our realities. Following this process will make us stronger and more evolved human beings so that we can navigate change more effectively and arrive at positive social, economic, and environmental outcomes.

Journaling / Meditation Questions

1. Think of a problem in your world. Who do you think is responsible for it? Who do you think is responsible for the solution? Did you include yourself in that list? Why or why not?

2. Do you feel isolated in your efforts or responsibilities to help solve the world's problems? Do you feel supported by others? Why or why not?

3. If your sole responsibility was for your own thoughts, feelings, words and actions, and you focused your attention on those exclusively, do you think we could still solve the world's problems?

4. What thoughts, feelings, words, and actions do you contribute to shaping our collective mental model of the world? Are they broadening our collective perspective or narrowing it?

Common Questions & Answers

Question 1: Can one be happy all the time, no matter what is going on around them?

Answer: Those who are happy all the time are suppressing their emotions and are in denial. We are constantly reacting to our external environment. Not everything that will happen to us will be positive. Our responses will reflect how we perceive what is going on around us. Our task is to process our emotional response to our external environment. We can become happy over time even in adverse conditions; but we cannot do that until we fully process our reality first.

Question 2: Is it possible to live without judgments, expectations and/or assumptions?

Answer: Our judgments, expectations and assumptions are the backbone of our mental model of the world. Without them we would not be able to navigate reality whatsoever. However, our mental model will be partially wrong and easily dated—as such, our judgments are unlikely to be fully correct, our expectations will not always be met, and our assumptions can be false. It is our task to update our mental model (including our judgments, expectations and assumptions) by seeking to understand our reality better.

Question 3: Can both discomfort and joy be legitimate motivating forces?

Answer: Discomfort can only be a motivating force to the extent it causes us to acknowledge reality and recalibrate our mental model. To the extent we feel discomfort in a given situation, our emotions are signaling to us that we need to take steps in a different direction. Our next steps are best taken out of joy as a motivating force, rather than out of fear of our discomfort. Joy is an emotion signaling our intrinsic motivation to move forward and is most aligned with meeting our needs.

Question 4: Isn't our brain designed for solving our problems?

Answer: Our brain is only designed to help us determine what our next steps should be given our current reality. Our brain can only make decisions based on our beliefs and assumptions about the world, which are based on the past and are subject to being outdated at any given moment. It is unfair to expect our brain to solve problems it cannot possibly solve without the input of our senses and emotions each step along the way. Our senses and emotions are designed to help us determine the state of our reality at any given moment and work to update our mental model over time.

Resources and Inspiration for this Book

Activities That Help Open Our Minds

The idea of journaling three pages comes from Julia Cameron, The Artists Way: A Spiritual Path to Higher Creativity (25th Anniversary Edition) (Tarcher Perigee 2006).

The practice of asking yourself what you would do differently if you accepted something as true comes from Teal Swan. She also describes how we frequently succumb to emotional denial in our attempts to avoid feeling anger, sadness and fear. "How to Thrive in a Crisis" Workshop (2020) *available at* https://tealswan.com/premium/.

Resolving internal conflicts requires having an internal dialogue with divergent aspects of yourself that do not agree with each other. Teal Swan, "The Mirror Event,"

Basel, Switzerland (2018), *available at* https://
tealswan.com/premium/.

The practice of culminating awareness for what is going
on inside of us and around us is discussed in Ellen J.
Langer, Mindfulness (25th Anniversary Edition), Da Capo
Press (2014).

The practice of feeling and expressing gratitude and
appreciation calms our nervous system, as described in
Louise Hay, *You Can Heal Your Life* (Hay House 1984).

Acceptance of Situations in Life

How we deal with changing circumstance will determine
our fate. Laurence Gonzales, *Deep Survival: Who Lives,
Who Dies, and Why* (W. W. Norton & Company 2004).

As studied in terminally ill patients, acceptance brings
us more peace, opens our minds, and calms our nervous
system. Documentary by Roslyn Dauber, entitled "A
New Understanding" (2017).

We are thinking and seeing our options most clearly when we are in a state of acceptance. Laurence Gonzales, *Deep Survival: Who Lives, Who Dies, and Why* (W. W. Norton & Company 2004).

Denial and Human Vulnerability

Human denial and resistance to change was captured in Franz Kafka's short story entitled, The Metamorphosis.

We beat our heads against reality when we assert that someone or a situation should change to meet our expectations. Katie Byron, *Loving What Is* (Harmony Books 2002).

Denial paralyzes our decision-making processes. Laurence Gonzales, *Deep Survival: Who Lives, Who Dies, and Why* (W. W. Norton & Company 2004).

Fear, Dangers of Fear-Based Decision-Making

Facing our fears requires gazing at them in the same way we would gaze into the eyes of a lover. Advice of

Credo Mutwa, as recounted by Linda Tucker in *Mystery of the White Lions* at 39 (Hay House 2010).

In a fear-based society, people will try to shame us into making decisions based on our fears. Anita Moorjani, "The Power of Suggestibility" YouTube (June 25, 2021).

Fear-based decision making leads to behavior that is not in our best interest or the best interest of others. Robin Dreeke with Cameron Stauth, "Sizing People Up: A Veteran FBI Agent's User Manual for Behavior Prediction," Penguin Publishing Group (2020).

Our Internal Navigation System

Our common set of needs was identified in Shalom H. Schwartz, "Basic Human Values: An Overview," in *Basic Human Values: Theory, Methods, and Applications* (The Hebrew University of Jerusalem 2006).

How our brains and biology perceive a situation, model the world, and respond to it has been documented in Lisa Feldman Barrett, "The Theory of Constructed

Emotion: An Active Inference Account of Interoception and Categorization," 12 *Social Cognitive and Affective Neuroscience* 1 pp. 1-23 (Jan 2017) (summarizing the literature).

Our beliefs form our internal logic. Andreas Moritz, *Lifting the Veil of Duality* (Ener-Chi Wellness Press 2010).

Emotions, Role of Emotions in our Navigation System

Connecting to our emotions helps brings us closer to acceptance. Rosalind Watts, et. al., "Patients' Accounts of Increased 'Connectedness' and 'Acceptance' After Psilocybin for Treatment-Resistant Depression," 57 *Journal of Humanistic Psychology* 5, 520-564 (2017).

Digesting emotions viscerally is a meditation practice discussed in Peter Fairfield, *Deep Happy: How to Get There and Always Find Your Way Back* (Red Wheel/ Weiser 2012).

Suppression of emotional energy leads to trauma. Bessel van der Kolk, *The Body Keeps the Score: Brain*

Mind and Body in the Healing of Trauma (Penguin Books 2014).

Emotions are a key aspect of our internal guidance system. Lisa Feldman Barrett, "The Theory of Constructed Emotion: An Active Inference Account of Interoception and Categorization," 12 *Social Cognitive and Affective Neuroscience* 1 pp. 1-23 (Jan 2017).

Mindset, Creativity, Flow

We perform better when we are open to the possibility that our capacities are constantly evolving. Carol Dweck, *Mindset; The New Psychology of Success* (Ballantine Books 2016)

We are most creative and most in the flow when we let go of our expectations and just have fun. Mihaly Csikszentmihalyi, *Flow: the Psychology of Optimal Experience* (Harper & Row 1990).

The modern concept of productivity has its roots in American slavery. Mehrsa Baradaran, "Mortgaging the

Future: The North-South rift led to a piecemeal system of bank regulation — with dangerous consequences" in *The 1619 Project of The New York Times Magazine* 31-38 (Aug. 18, 2019).

The Physical Body

The ungrounded personality archetype is exemplified in "Woody Allen Montage," YouTube (July 18, 2012).

The grounded personality archetype is exemplified in "Best of - Arnold Schwarzenegger" YouTube (November 11, 2018).

Physically shaking off traumatic experiences helps heal the nervous system. David Berceli, *The Revolutionary Trauma Release Process* (Namaste Publishing 2020).

There are exercises a person can do to induce tremors that recalibrate the nervous system, which are called Tension and Trauma Release Exercises. *See* traumaprevention.com

Acute and chronic exposures to toxic chemicals can distort our thoughts and emotions. Joanna Malaczynski, *Silent Winter: Our Chemical World & Chronic Illness* (Algora Publishing 2021).

When our nervous system is calm, we make better decisions. Stephen W. Porges "The polyvagal theory: new insights into adaptive reactions of the autonomic nervous system." 76 *Cleveland Clinic Journal of Medicine* Supplement 2 at S86 - S90 (April 2009).

Working With / Understanding Others

Many problems arise or persist due to a failure to understand other people. Marshall Rosenberg, *Non-Violent Communication San Francisco Workshop* (April 2000), *available on* YouTube *at* https://www.youtube.com/watch?v=I7TONauJGfc&t=6s.

It is important to learn to communicate to others what we need. Marshall Rosenberg, *Nonviolent Communication* (PuddleDancer Press 2003).

For a comic discussion of how we talk ourselves out of opportunity based on what we think others will have to say, see Joanna Malaczynski, "What I Learned About Innovation from Practicing Law," Disruptor League (January 20, 2019), available at https://www.disruptorleague.com/blog/2019/01/20/what-i-learned-about-innovation-from-practicing-law/.

Effective problem-solving requires active listening to the people who are experiencing the brunt of the problem, as illustrated by this IDEO Case Study, "A New Employment Venture to Increase Customer Engagement and Financial Security," available at https://www.ideo.com/case-study/a-new-employment-venture-to-increase-customer-engagement-and-financial-security.

About the Author

Joanna Malaczynski-Moore left her career as an attorney to focus her energies on solving the world's sustainability problems. Even though she joined the ranks of professionals who were excited about making the world a better place, she found that—like most of her colleagues—she was not able to create change because we are largely resistant to it. Joanna turned to spirituality and other disciplines to make sense of this reality. She learned that our capacity to solve problems and move forward in life is dependent upon successful use of our internal navigation system. This book is a culmination of what she has learned about our internal navigation system, how we create positive change, and the obstacles we face along the way. Joanna regularly relies upon the processes laid out in this book to help her navigate her own life challenges. She lives with multiple chemical sensitivity, an invisible disability caused by toxic chemical exposures.